Southw

and Halai..

on old picture postcards

David Ottewell

1. Greetings postcard published by A. and G. Taylor, a London firm, and posted from Southwell in September 1907.

£3.50

Designed and Published by
Reflections of a Bygone Age,
Keyworth, Nottingham

1992

Reprinted 2003

2. The "Admiral Rodney" was built in the middle of the 18th century, taking its name from the famous sailor who in 1780 defeated the Spanish fleet at Cape St. Vincent. This is one of many cards in the book published by Howard Barrett of Southwell.

All rights reserved. No part of this book may be reproduced or transmitted in any form or by any means, electronic or mechanical, including photocopying, recording or by any information storage and retrieval system, without permission in writing from the Publisher.

Printed by
Adlard Print and Typesetting Services,
Ruddington, Notts.

THE "ADMIRAL RODNEY" LIVERY
STABLES & MOTOR GARAGE SOUTHWELL
A MERRYFIELD PROPRIETOR.

3. The carriageway to the side of the "Admiral Rodney". This has now been incorporated into the hotel, forming the entrance to the bar. When this card was published about 1908, A. Merryfield was the hotel proprietor.

Southwell. The Old Saracen's Head

4. The "Saracen's Head" features in the right foreground, with the Assembly Rooms next to it. These were built in 1805 by a local architect and stonemason called Ingleman. Originally, the first floor contained a ballroom and musicians' gallery. The ornate columns have now been blocked in, and the premises used as extra accommodation for the hotel.

INTRODUCTION

Southwell is a very attractive town lying in rolling countryside, and even to-day in the hustle and bustle of late 20th century life it has an air of tranquility. It has experienced an interesting and varied history, having played host to royalty from Charles I to our present Queen, as well as men of history and literature such as Oliver Cromwell and the poet Byron.

Although dominated by the Minster, Southwell has many other interesting buildings and thankfully, unlike in many other places, the majority of these remain today, although often altered in appearance or usage.

The name Southwell is thought to derive from the number of wells in the area thus South-well as opposed to Nor-well, a village towards Newark. The pronunciation of the name, however, is in dispute even amongst locals, many of whom say "suth'ell".

Postcards were first introduced into Great Britain in 1894, but it wasn't until Post Office rules were changed in 1902 so that the picture could take up the whole of the front of the card and the message and address the reverse that postcards really came into their own.

The so-called 'Golden Age' of postcards continued until the First World War with upwards of three million cards being sent daily. Even after this time, cards were sent in large numbers.

Southwell was lucky to have two photographers, the prolific Howard Barrett, and Alfred J. Loughton, who produced cards of the town and the surrounding area. There were also other publishers of cards in Southwell such as G.A. Padgett, Miss Playstead and T.A. Maltby. Additionally national postcard publishers like Frith of Reigate and Photochrom of Tunbridge Wells took photographs and produced cards of Southwell.

The illustrations in this book are chosen from the wealth of images to be found on these postcards and provide an opportunity to step back into earlier times in this century.

David Ottewell
September 1992

Front cover: A cycling party outside the "Saracen's Head" on a Howard Barrett postcard.
Back cover (top): The "Crown Hotel" and Grammar School, Southwell, on a 1920s postcard published by Miss Playstead, 'Milliner and fancy establishment'.
　　　　　　　(bottom): Southwell Minster in rural setting on a card by Howard Barrett.

Acknowledgements: Thanks to Tim Farr for the loan of cards 1, 13, 27, 31, 36, 38, 55 and 57.

5. Situated in a prominent place in Southwell, the "Saracen's Head" has long been a meeting venue for local groups. The Rufford Hunt is featured on this c.1908 card by Barrett.

KING CHARLES 1st LEAVING THE OLD COURT-YARD OF THE SARACEN'S HEAD INN, SOUTHWELL, NOTTS. 1646

6. Most famous visitor to the inn was Charles I, who dined here in May 1646 before surrendering to the Scottish Commissioners, whose army was based at nearby Kelham Hall. At the time the inn was known as "the King's Arms". This card was published by a North Yorkshire firm.

7. View in the "Saracen's Head" courtyard showing a sign for a Midland Railway parcel receiving office. This card was published by Alfred J. Loughton of Southwell, a whitesmith and cycle agent whose premises were on Queen Street.

8. Manchester House, the second shop along from the hotel, was built in Georgian times. Its demise came in 1950 with the need for road widening to provide easier access to and from Queen Street. The message on the card, published by A. Wood (bookseller, Southwell) and posted from the town in September 1924, reads *"I have managed to leave Peter whilst I got to Southwell, with a promise of a banana."*

9. This postcard of King Street by the Cotswold Publishing Co. dates from around 1908 when the shop centre left with the boy and wheelbarrow outside was owned by John James Bates, grocer and china, glass and earthenware dealer. He was also an agent for W. & A. Gilbey, wine and spirit merchant.

10. Miss Playstead, who had a milliners and fancy goods shop on King Street, published this unusual view looking down from the top of the street. It was posted in August 1920.

11. The photographer here has captured a lively King Street full of action. On the right is the Central Stores and, two buildings along from this, the millinery shop of Louisa Sheard. Almost opposite is John Mills and Sons, bootmakers. The card, by an unknown publisher, was posted at Southwell on 26th December 1910.

12. The "Crown Inn", dating from 1820, is on the right of the picture, with Manchester House in the middle distance. This card was actually posted from Beeston and sent to Derby in February 1910.

13. A much later card of King Street, posted at Newark in August 1954, with a view taken from outside the "Saracen's Head". On the right is the National Provincial Bank.

14. Another 1950s view, looking in the other direction. The postcard was published by
T.A. Maltby, whose shop can be seen on the left, next to the bank featured on illus. 13.

15. Church Street, seen from the entrance to the "Saracen's Head", on a card posted
in September 1949 and published by the famous photographic firm Frith of Reigate.
The pair of local schoolboys are about to pass the National Provincial Bank. The writer
says of Southwell *"it really is a sweet little place."*

16. Another of Howard Barrett's postcards. He had a studio on Station Road, and liked to advertise the fact that he had been patronised by King Edward VII. This view is from the bottom of Church Street, looking back towards the Minster.

17. This card by Frith, looking up Church Street, gives an idea of the size and style of some of the town's houses and gardens.

Nottingham & Notts Bank, Southwell.

18. The premises of Nottingham and Notts Bank on Church Street, seen here on a c.1916 Barrett card, are still used as a bank. Manager when this photo was taken was Charles L. Maltby.

SOUTHWELL. THE MANOR HOUSE.

19. The Burgage Manor House is seen here on a snowy winter's day about 1912. It has had a long and varied history: built in the 18th century, it was in 1803 that the poet Byron's mother rented the house, and while at Harrow and Cambridge, Byron spent his vacations here. However, he apparently failed to appreciate the town. Postcard by Barrett.

BURGAGE MANOR YOUTH HOSTEL

20. Printed by the Y.H.A. (North Midland Region), this card shows the manor in one of its later uses as a youth hostel. It also served as a girls' school and a soldiers' convalescent home as well as a private residence.

Southwell,
Burgage, Byron's House

21. The freeholders of the Manor of Burgage held ancient rights to graze their animals on the green. Frith of Reigate published this card with a very pleasant rural flavour.

BURGAGE GREEN, SOUTHWELL

22. Posted in 1923 from Southwell to Bristol, this card published by G. Padgett of Southwell shows the side of Burgage where the House of Correction, with its notorious treadmill, was situated. The last convict left in 1880, and a lace factory was established in the premises.

Southwell War Memorial.

23. The war memorial on the Burgage commemorates the ninety local men who lost their lives in the Great War. On the left is the 'Burgage' house itself; ownership of this entitled the occupant to a vote in Parliamentary elections after the 1832 Reform Act.

24. Cauldwell's began milling at their premises near the railway station in 1851, but suffered damaging fires in both 1867 and 1893. The seven-storey water tower was a later addition; it included an automatic sprinkler system. Milling ceased in 1969. To the right is the stationmaster's house and the signal box.

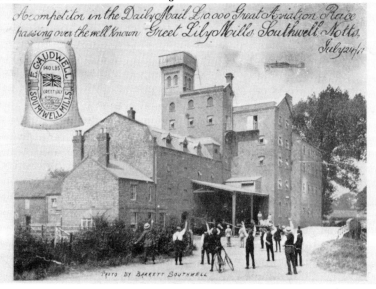

25. The Greet Lily Mills are situated next to the River Greet, which supplied the water to power the water wheel. This postcard by Barrett commemorates the Daily Mail Air Race of 24th July 1911 and claims to show a competitor passing over the mill. The card was posted to Wath-on-Dearne in July 1913, and the reverse claims the firm won the Nottinghamshire Baker Cup in 1907, 1908 and 1909.

Photographed and Published by Howard Barrett, Southwell.   Thrice Patronised by His late Majesty King Edward VII.
H Co. 8TH NOTTS & DERBY T.F., *leaving Southwell for Active Service, August 7th, 1914.*

26. Howard Barrett captured on postcard some of the local men who were to serve in the Great War, leaving Southwell for active service on 7th August 1914. They are seen here almost at the station with its entrance on the left of the picture. The "Newcastle Arms", which many would surely have preferred as their destination, is on the right.

27. The caption on this card by Barrett claims these are 'Mexican mules for the war'. At the entrance to the station yard is the "Newcastle Arms", built in the 1860s when it was appropriately known as the "New Inn".

The Railway Station, Southwe[ll]

28. Southwell's first railway station, made of wood,
2½-mile single-track branch line which joined the N[
Mansfield and a stone station erected. When this pos[
just four trains ran to Mansfield each day (with an extr[
to Rolleston in 1959, and final closure of the goods l[

by the Midland Railway Company in 1847 at the head of a
-Lincoln line at Rolleston. In 1871 the line was extended to
sted from Southwell to Lincoln in July 1912) was published,
hursdays). The last passenger train to Mansfield was in 1929,
n 1964.

29. Howard Barrett postcard featuring the railway smash at Southwell on 25th June 1907.

30. Moore's garage — an advertising card published by Barrett.

GRAMMAR SCHOOL, SOUTHWELL

31. The Grammar School in Southwell was established by Act of Parliament in 1543. Richard Ingleman, who was responsible for the Assembly Rooms, also designed this building about 1819. The school moved in 1964 when the need for more space and modern facilities necessitated a change.

HILL HOUSE. A BOARDING HOUSE OF THE
MINSTER GRAMMAR SCHOOL. SOUTHWELL.

CA.036.A.

32. Jack Braithwaite of Leeds published this aerial postcard view of Hill House, used in the 1950s as a boarding house for the Minster Grammar School. It was originally built by Rev. John Thomas Becher in 1802.

Southwell Fire Brigade.

33. According to a 1908 directory, the fire engine house was situated on Queen Street, with Robert Ellis as superintendent. He controlled a force of 8 firemen, all of whom have turned out here for Howard Barrett's photographer.

South Muskham Prebend, Southwell.

34. Southwell has a number of prebends. This is the South Muskham one (now used as a home for elderly people), featured on a 1960s postcard by T.A. Maltby.

35. Easthorpe's claim to fame is that in a cottage garden here, Miss Mary Brailsford planted an apple pip which grew into a new strain of apple. It was named Bramley after a subsequent owner of the cottage, Matthew Bramley. This postcard was published by Frith, and posted to Chilwell in June 1922.

Holy Trinity Church, Southwell.

36. Holy Trinity Church, an impressive building in early English style, has a 150-foot spire. It contains seating for 400 worshippers. Designed by Hadfield and costing £4,000, it was consecrated on 31st March 1846. Another Barrett card, sent to Pleasley in April 1907.

Westhorpe, Southwell,

37. Westhorpe on a Howard Barrett postcard, postally used from Nottingham in 1907. The "Lord Nelson" pub is on the left.

S 12962   WESTGATE, SOUTHWELL.

38. Westgate, with a horse and cart conveying Mosedale's prize bread (supplied daily) on a postcard published by A. Wood of Southwell.

39. This ornate entrance to the recreation ground was erected in memory of the local people who gave their lives in the two world wars. Card published c.1960 by T.A. Maltby from his Market Place shop.

40. A much earlier view of the recreation ground by Barrett, sent from Southwell on Christmas Eve 1906. It shows a gathering with a band setting up on the right.

Southwell City Football Team, 1910-11.

WINNERS OF THE NEWARK & DISTRICT LEAGUE CHALLENGE CUP.

41. Southwell City Football team 1910-11 when they won the Newark and District League Challenge Cup.

SOUTHWELL THURSDAY F.C. 1911-12.

42. The Thursday F.C. 1911-12 on a Barrett postcard.

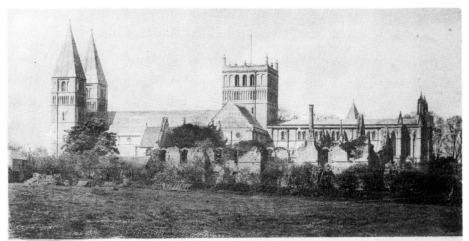

Southwell Cathedral.

The Woodbury Series, No. 284.

43. In 956 Oskytel, Archbishop of York, founded a church in Southwell, its purpose being to serve the southern area of the See of York. None of this church survives, but the principle had been established. Today's Minster was built in three phases during the 12th and 13th centuries, though since then the ravages of time and fire have necessitated repairs and restorations. The Minster's most prominent feature, the twin west spires, were removed in 1801 because they were thought unsafe. A pair of new spires in a similar design was built in 1880 and gained the name 'pepper-pots'. In 1884 the Southwell diocese was formed, elevating the Minster to the status of a Cathedral. This postcard by Eyre and Spottiswoode was published around 1905.

44. Set amongst the aged splendour of the Minster buildings, the Bishop's Manor, home of the Bishop of Southwell, was only completed in 1907. The Great Hall of the Archbishop's Palace originally occupied the site. Anonymously-published photographic card.

Funeral of The Bishop of Southwell, Sept. 3rd, 1904.

45. George Ridding, the first Bishop of Southwell, died in 1904 and was buried in the Minster on 3rd September. Barrett was naturally on hand to record the occasion.

ENTHRONEMENT OF THE BISHOP OF SOUTHWELL.   Dec. 8, 1904.

46. In December 1904 his successor, Dr. E. Hoskyns, was enthroned. This card was posted to Balderton in April 1905.

47. This Barrett card, posted to Radcliffe-on-Trent, shows the ceremony on 2nd February 1906 at which the Bishop of Southwell laid the foundation stone for the new Bishop's Manor, the building designed by W.D. Caroe and completed in the following year. *(see illus. 44).*

48. Seen here on the platform of Southwell station, the homecoming of the Bishop and his wife on 29th June 1907 attracted a welcoming committee of local people as well as the attentions of the station staff. Card by Barrett. *"Don't they all look happy in this picture?"* wrote the sender, posting it three days after the event.

49. As an important local personage, anything the Bishop of Southwell did attracted attention. Here he is seen with his wife and their new motor car — still something of a novelty in Edwardian times — at Wollaton Hall Gateway. The occasion was recorded by postcard publisher Montgomery.

50. Photographic Barrett postcard recording the presentation to Archdeacon and Mrs Richardson at Southwell on 31st January 1913.

STUDIO

1. HOW RHUBARB FARED
AND A LUMP OF SNOW.

2. SWEEPING THE SNOW
AWAY.

3. SCENE IN STATION
ROAD.

A SNOW STORM IN THE MONTH OF ROSES.

REMARKABLE SCENES AT SOUTHWELL, NOTTS. JUNE 10TH, 1912.

The storm started about 7 o'clock at night and in ten minutes time the streets presented the appearance of midwinter. Flakes of snow and ice fell as large as walnuts, cutting off garden produce and most of the garden entirely ruined. The storm was confined to the locality of Southwell, and such an occurence cannot be recalled by residents.

51. A freak snowstorm on 10th June 1912, when a 10-minute fall of hailstones at about 7 in the evening was so severe that local produce was damaged. Barrett card, posted to Fakenham on the 21st. *"I understand that you read of the terrible storm seen here on the 10th, so thought you would like to see this. I think it has rained nearly every day since you left ..."*

HALAM RD SOUTHWELL. 2

52. This card of Halam Road was sent from Southwell in September 1915 by a soldier. *"Am getting on ripping, you ought to be here but the physical drill would knock you out. Talk about chest. I am putting it on every day,"* he wrote to a friend in Heckmond-wike.

53. An ivy-covered Westhorpe Hall, General Warren's house when Miss Playstead published this card in the 1920s. Built in the 18th century, it is now a Grade II listed building, which in recent years has been turned into apartments.

54. Until 1646 Norwood Park was one of four episcopal parks around Southwell owned by the Archbishop of York. In 1646 a parliamentarian, Edward Cludd, purchased the land and built a house. This was demolished in 1760 by John Sutton and the present Hall was erected. Card by Howard Barrett.

PHOTOGRAPHED BY HOWARD BARRETT, SOUTHWELL, NOTTS.　THRICE PATRONISED BY HIS LATE MAJESTY KING EDWARD VII.

W.R.D.R.E. NORWOOD PARK. MAY 24, 1915.

55. In 1881 Mrs Lewis Starkey bought the Hall and Park, and it remains in the same family today. This card illustrates its use as a training camp for soldiers in the Great War. Barrett published it, and it was posted to Newark in July 1915.

56. Halam village and Wesleyan Chapel, 1½ miles from Southwell. The Chapel was built in 1896 at a cost of £250. Late 1930s card by Raphael Tuck of London.

EMPIRE DAY AT HALAM. NOTTS. 1914.   PHOTO, H. BARRETT, SOUTHWELL

57. Empire Day at Halam in 1914 on a photographic card by Barrett.

58. The "Plough Inn" at Halam, selling Worksop Ales, and a group of children on a rather wet day in the mid-1920s.

59. The Rufford Hounds outside the "Plough" at Halam on 11th January 1906 on a Barrett postcard.

60. Halam church with a selection of villagers assembled by Barrett. This card was posted at Southwell in October 1905.

61. 1960s card by A.W. Bourne of Leicester, featuring Halam Post Office, the "Waggon and Horses", and the "Plough".